# BEAUTIFUL BRITAIN

Published by VisitBritain Publishing, Thames Tower, Blacks Road, London W6 9EL

First published 2007

© British Tourist Authority (trading as VisitBritain) 2007

ISBN
978 0 7095 8397 4
Product code: IMAGES02

A CIP catalogue record for this book is available from the British Library.

All the photographs in *Beautiful Britain* were selected from VisitBritain's official online image library, Britain on View.

Editorial and design by Indigo 3 Publishing for VisitBritain Publishing.
Reprographics by CTT Limited.
Printed and bound in Dubai by Oriental Press.

Front cover: Horsey by John Miller

# BEAUTIFUL BRITAIN

# BEAUTIFUL BRITAIN

**B**eautiful Britain reveals the diversity of the coast and countryside of England, Scotland and Wales – from the sheltered harbours of Devon and Cornwall to the towering cliffs of Scotland and the sweeping, sandy bays of West Wales, and from the open marshes of East Anglia to the plunging valleys of Snowdonia and the snowy peaks of the Highlands.

Revealing how Britain changes from north to south and
from season to season, *Beautiful Britain* provides a panoramic
view of a small nation boasting a huge variety of natural
landscapes: atmospheric moors and imposing mountains,
sparkling lakes and tranquil beaches, shaded woods and
open pastures.

Taken from Britain on View, VisitBritain's own image library,
the stunning selection of photographs in this book gives
a unique insight into the landscape of an island nation.
*Beautiful Britain* also includes a useful index for all of the
places and destinations featured.

*One cannot collect all the
beautiful shells on the beach;
one can collect only a few;
and they are more beautiful
if they are few.*

ANNE MORROW LINDBERGH

*My heart's in the Highlands,
my heart is not here;
My heart's in the Highlands
a-chasing the deer;
Chasing the wild deer,
and following the roe,
My heart's in the Highlands,
wherever I go.*

**ROBERT BURNS**

p22 River Avon, Wiltshire

*Nothing is lovelier than moving water,*
*The diamond element, innumerable jewel,*
*Brittle and splintering under the sharp sun,*
*Yet softer than doves' feathers, and more smooth*
*Than down of swan.*

**GERALD BULLETT**

*What are young men
to rocks and mountains?*

**JANE AUSTEN**

# BEAUTIFUL BRITAIN

*Generations pass while some trees stand,*
*and old families last not three oaks.*

**SIR THOMAS BROWNE**

*Break, break, break,*
*On thy cold grey stones, O sea!*
*And I would that my tongue could utter*
*The thoughts that arise in me.*

**ALFRED LORD TENNYSON**

p43 Cissbury Ring, West Sussex
p44~45 Wastwater, Cumbria
p46 Rhoscolyn, Isle of Anglesey

*This precious stone set in a silver sea,*
*Which serves it in the office of a wall,*
*Or as a moat defensive to a house,*
*Against the envy of less happier lands,*
*This blessèd plot, this earth,*
*this realm, this England.*

**WILLIAM SHAKESPEARE**

p62~63 Standon, Hertfordshire
p64~65 Seven Sisters, East Sussex

*I had been dreaming about a lighthouse. It is such a potent image; practical, because lives depend on it, and at the same time, utterly romantic, this lonely building on the cusp of land and sea, sending out light into the darkness.*

**JEANETTE WINTERSON**

p74 & 75 Southwold, Suffolk

*Rocks, torrents, gulfs,*
*and shapes of giant size,*
*And glittering cliffs on cliffs,*
*and fiery ramparts rise.*

**JAMES BEATTIE**

93

*Starred forget-me-nots smile sweetly,*
*Ring, bluebells, Ring!*
*Winning eye and heart completely,*
*Sing, robin, Sing!*

**SARAH FOSTER DAVIS**

# Index

# Image Acknowledgements

| | |
|---|---|
| Angel, David | 10 |
| Britainonview.com | 14, 16, 38, 40, 44, 56 |
| Cornish, Joe | 18, 20, 24, 28, 36, 75, 83, 84, 86, 92, 94, 95, 96, 102 |
| Edwards, Rod | 32, 54, 62, 68, 74, 88, 100 |
| Gough, Graham | 50 |
| Guy, VK / Guy, Mike | 66, 72 |
| Guy, VK / Guy, Paul | 112 |
| Hall, David | 98 |
| Hardley, Dennis | 55, 90, 108 |
| Hicks, Nigel | 48, |
| Lewis, Steve | 26, 46, 80 |
| Miller, John | 4, 105 |
| Sayer, Howard | 60 |
| Sellman, David | 8, 22, 23, 31, 34, 43, 52, 58, 64, 107, 110 |
| Shaw, Duncan | 82, 106 |
| Watson, Richard | 70, 76 |
| Weston, Colin | 12, 78 |

All the photographs featured in Beautiful Britain are supplied by
britainonview.com, the official online image library of VisitBritain.

**Britain**onview

# Quotation Acknowledgements

13        Anne Morrow Lindbergh (1906-2001), Gift From the Sea by Anne Morrow Lindbergh, published by Chatto & Windus. Reprinted by permission of The Random House Group Ltd

21        Robert Burns (1759-1796), 'My Heart's in the Highlands' (1790)

30        Gerald Bullett (1893-1958), Collected Poems (1959)

35        Jane Austen (1775-1817), Pride and Prejudice, Penguin Classics (31 December, 2002)

42        Sir Thomas Browne (1605-1682), Hydriotaphia (Urn Burial 1658) ch. 5

47        Alfred Lord Tennyson (1809-1892), 'Break, Break, Break' (1842)

65        William Shakespeare (1564-1616), Richard II (1595) act 2, sc. 3, 1.2

73        Jeanette Winterson (1959-present), Lighthousekeeping, Harcourt (11 April, 2005)

87        James Beattie (1735-1803), Poetical Works (Works by James Beattie), Thoemmes Continuum (April 2001)


Particular thanks go to Jeanette Winterson and Random House Group Ltd.

Every attempt has been made to contact current copyright holders of quoted material.
Any errors or omissions will be rectified in future editions or reprints.